Sleep, Nap, Doze, Work Function

A Proposal To Gain More From Power Savings In Computing

Edward Seymour

Sleep, Nap, Doze, Work Function

A Proposal To Gain More From Power Savings In Computing

Edward Seymour

Copyright 2016

Edward Seymour

ISBN 978-1-365-43262-0

This text is dedicated to revealing a new paradigm which can radically change effectiveness of computing

Table of Contents

About the author

I began my study of computer architecture with intel 8085 and motorola 68000 long ago. My studies continued within IBM with the IBM PC, 370 VMS and VM operating systems and even involved a study of pdp 11/44 from digital equipment corporation. From there began a journey with PowerPC architecture. Throughout this time it became increasingly important to manage workload and correspondingly manage power.

I have survived testing many forms of power management with an insistence on the part of design teams that power is a given, assumed constant, never reflected logically in any circuit, is the only way to go. Suffice it to say, I have numerous experiences that suggest this is a short sighted and ineffective simplification. In the interest of time, I will defer this discussion to yet another text.

Background

With continued shrinks of device sizes in current circuits, the term leakage current has become an accepted "fact". This argument is predicated on the use of CMOS circuits combine with the notion that power is not eligible as a term in a boolean expression. Given this notion, leakage happens and produces unwanted power use. This created the need for Sleep, Nap, Doze as new states for a computer.

Crux Of My Idea

Since we already have the aforementioned states available in computing, I suggest we harvest a greater work function from them by re-arranging tasks which prepare for entry into each of these states such that we more closely emulate the efficacy that we as humans gain from these activities. Thus far, in computing, these functions have been viewed as non-work, forced by over consumption of power relative to performance. My supposition is these activities represent different gradients of higher level thought when structured correctly.

Sleep Which Includes REM Cycles

This is a contemporary view of how we sleep. As applied to computing the harvest during sleep relies on a few elements.

1) Set in your mind a goal of a consuming task, large goal (perform a cache flush – write this to disk for later retreival, otherwise put, perform a checkpoint of state)

2) Identify background tasks performed by agents involving

   research state of art techniques

   survey the surroundings

   perform trial and error

   (these tasks are allowed to run during your sleep)

☐ Be certain to explicitly create a rule which defines the tasks which are to be summarily dismissed (kill -kill) as they need to be removed from running memory, freed from any disk (DCBZ)

☐ During sleep, ignore any interruptions until wake up call

☐ Upon wake up, perform restore of state and query results of allowed background tasks

Associated Rules

1. All memory and disk allocation for any of the sleep queries should be using linked lists for data gathered

2. Each list should be keyed by privileged process number

3. Each query should be formed as a SQL or perl if exists query

4. For higher level thinking, all procedures that lack process permission for this task are immediately killed

Extension to Nap

This next form of sleep allows more tasks to remain and would fall into this same framework aforementioned. I would say that Nap would become the equivalent of a survey course where the number of allowed processes is expanded as the vectors of exploration. The main outcome of Nap is to determine if it is a viable concept. The point of this is to do a step wise refinement of a course to be undertaken.

Representation of Doze

In sleep, this is the most attentive and directed effort. This represents the act of rote practice. This is where boundary conditions are crisply understood. One does not question why but focuses on committing to memory, how. The associated learning is simply a procedure to practice a skill with repitition. It can be expressed in computer language as repeat until (condition reached) or iterate while (goal still not achieved) where steps to be performed are prescribed by a master and condition or goal, ie measure of completion is also enumerated o set by master.

Illustrations Of Master/Apprentice

In order to fully understand examples of Sleep, Nap, Doze, I performed a simple search using baidu.

Single Example Of Doze in Android

For example doze in android is defined to be
http://news.yesky.com/460/69643960.shtml by one source

Illustrative Idea Of Computer Sleep Within Linux

Sleep has the following suggested prescription as defined In linux, a father of Android.

How Android Takes A Nap

An illustrated definition of Nap under android produces
http://www.coolapk.com/apk/net.jzhang.powernap

Analogy Between Contemporary Prescribed Method And Operating System

Computing, as it is known is performed under a set of rules much like, we, as people are constrained by laws, international, regional and local, computers are deemed to be mindless servants under strict prescribed rules.

Instruction Set Defines Core Tasks Inside Operational Framework (Operating System)

Suffice it to say, language provides nouns, verbs, adjectives, adverbs and rules for assembly or expression of thought. Some ideas are best conveyed in latin, as above. Others, most effective in Chinese (Mandarin). Still others best conveyed in essence of french. The list goes on in example of written or vocal language expression.

Current Operational Models Need New Instructions

I suggest, do not call these new instructions by the name extension. They can be formed in API, Function Call, macro assembly but their introduction and application should simplify or add elegance to current methods, not be formed as a complex idea (modern form of bandaid or hack) but rather a simply understood, broadly accepted notion.

New Macro Assembly Instruction Sets To Be Formed

In order to readily implement vast improvements in computing under the auspices of Sleep, Nap, Doze, elegance and intuitive advances can be achieved simply. This does not require new vernacular in the strict sense but simpler phrasing with greater precision.

Perl Instruction Set

This language operates with very little overhead today but conceptually is under utilized. Such notions of "if(exists X) {} combined with linked lists formed using "$nameyourvariable{naturalindex}=(storedorobservedvalue)" is one of the most elegant (simple) ideas which simply requires fundamental linked list construction in hardware.

My suggestion is offer the entire dictionary of perl as a set of APIs so perl becomes native, period, end of story.

Awk Instruction Set

Same argument applies here. Same approach suggested. Different gains including ease of column manipulations, transforms, essential queries and reconstruction or formation of reports

Grep Instruction Set

Again, native instruction constructed of macro assembly. Best used with Awk or Sed

Sed Instruction Set

This animal offers unique functions ill-understood but still used by me. How bad can it be to code the macro assembly of this?

Challenge: Provide These Assembly Macros

Realistically if this takes more than a few hours to construct, my point is lost.

Idea Is Elegance==Simplicity and NOT Complexity

Acknowledgments

I owe a special gratitude my wife for her understanding, support and intellectual exchange. Notable mention would go to countless people I encounter daily.

Conceptual Understanding

I will open with this disclaimer. I am trained as an engineer who has studied Microelectronics, Photo Science, Economics, Physics, computer science and Business. Thus, I did not take classes in "sleep" but have had significant involvement in programs where power management schemes have been devised and my responsibility has been to test them.

It is my belief that to properly teach a topic requires a conceptual understanding of it.

Intended Audience

This book is intended for anyone who has used a computer and become frustrated. It equally applies to those who spend tireless hours to try and make computers think more in lines like us.

Think Bigger

Reduce Scope

Reduce, Recycle, Reuse

Study From A Master